Penguins

WE BOTH READ®

Parent's Introduction

Whether your child is a beginning reader, a reluctant reader, or an eager reader, this book offers a fun and easy way to encourage and help your child in reading.

Developed with reading education specialists, **We Both Read** books invite you and your child to take turns reading aloud. You read the left-hand pages of the book, and your child reads the right-hand pages—which have easier text written at a specific reading level. The result is a wonderful new reading experience and faster reading development!

You may find it helpful to read the entire book aloud yourself the first time, then invite your child to participate the second time. As you read, try to make the story come alive by reading with expression. This will help to model good fluency.

In some books, a few challenging words are introduced in the parent's text with **bold** lettering. Pointing out and discussing these words can help to build your child's reading vocabulary. If your child is a beginning reader, it may be helpful to run a finger under the text as each of you reads. To help show whose turn it is, a blue dot ● comes before text for you to read, and a red star ★ comes before text for your child to read.

If your child struggles with a word, you can encourage "sounding it out," but keep in mind that this will not help with all words because some words don't follow phonetic patterns.

What is this word?

Can you try to sound it out?

You can help with breaking down the sounds of the letters or syllables, but if your child becomes too frustrated, it is usually best to simply say the word.

While reading together, try to help your child understand what is being read. It can help to stop every few pages to ask questions about the text and check if there are any words your child doesn't understand. After you finish the book, ask a few more questions or discuss what you've read together. Rereading this book multiple times may also help your child to read with more ease and understanding.

Most importantly, remember to praise your child's efforts and keep the reading fun. Keep the tips above in mind, but don't worry about doing everything right. Simply sharing the enjoyment of reading together will increase your child's reading skills and help to start your child on a lifetime of reading enjoyment!

Penguins

A We Both Read Book
Level 2
Guided Reading Level: K

With special thanks to Emma Kocina, biologist at the California Academy of Sciences, for her review of the information in this book

Text Copyright © 2024 by Sindy McKay
Use of most photographs provided by iStock and Dreamstime.
Use of the following photographs provided by the Australian Antarctic Division:
Page 27, upper left: Emperor penguins at Auster Rookery, 2008 © Garry Miller/ Australian Antarctic Division; Page 36, upper right: Huddle of emperor penguins near Mawson research station, 2022 © Troy Henderson/Australian Antarctic Division

We Both Read® is a trademark of Treasure Bay, Inc.

Published by
Treasure Bay, Inc.
PO Box 519
Roseville, CA 95661 USA

Printed in China

Library of Congress Control Number: 2023910559

ISBN: 978-1-60115-376-0

Visit us online at:
WeBothRead.com

PR-10-23-Leo

Table of Contents

Gentoo penguins
Antarctica

● Penguins, with their black and white "tuxedo" look and funny way of walking, are popular animals often featured in movies, television, and cartoons. They are most often shown in snowy locations, but not all penguins live in the snow.

Rockhopper penguin

★ Some types of penguins live in much warmer places. These African penguins, for example, live on the sunny beaches of South Africa.

Where else do penguins live?

3

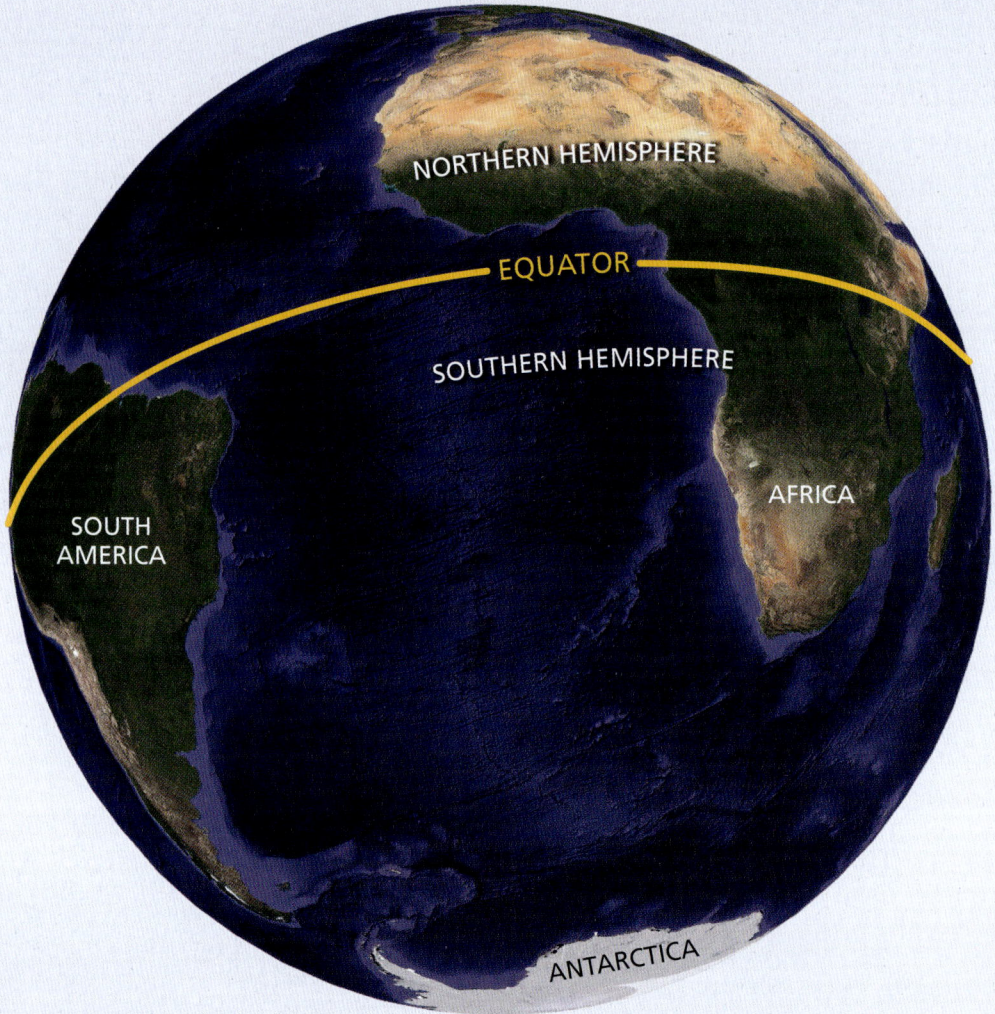

- The Earth is a sphere which is often divided on maps by an imaginary line called the **equator** (ee-QUAY-tore). Everything located south of the **equator** is in the Southern Hemisphere (HEM-iss-feer). This is where almost all penguins live. It is extremely rare to find a penguin in the Northern Hemisphere.

Polar bears
Arctic

★ Polar bears and penguins are sometimes shown together in movies and cartoons. But in real life, these animals will never meet. Penguins live south of the **equator**. Polar bears live far north of the equator.

Gentoo penguins
Antarctica

5

Emperor penguins
Antarctica

●   There are eight types of penguins that live on the ice and snow of Antarctica. Perhaps the most recognizable species is the mighty emperor penguin.

   Several other types of penguins live where it is much warmer. Galapagos (ge-LAP-e-gose) penguins live in the warmest climate. They can be found on islands off the **ocean** coast of Ecuador (EH-kwi-dore) in South America. Temperatures here can reach 80 degrees.

Galapagos penguin
Galapagos Islands, Ecuador

Rockhopper penguins
Falkland Islands, South America

★ All penguins live near the **ocean**. They spend most of their time in the water. This is where they look for and find the food they eat. Penguins eat krill, squid, and fish.

Bigfin reef squid

Antarctic krill

7

Krill swarm

Krill
close up

- A single krill is no bigger than a fingernail, so a penguin must eat a lot of them to make a meal. Fortunately, krill travel in swarms—sometimes made up of several million of them!

  Penguins often dive deep to find their food. While humans can dive no more than 60 feet without special equipment, an emperor penguin can dive down more than 1,500 feet. That's like taking an elevator from the top of a 100-story skyscraper all the way down to the ground floor!

Emperor penguin

Humboldt penguin swallowing a fish

★ People who study penguins have discovered they have very little sense of taste. It doesn't seem to matter because they swallow their food whole.

Penguins have small spines inside their mouth and on their tongue. These are called papillae (pe-PILL-lay). The spines grip a slippery fish and send it down the throat.

Humboldt penguin

Papillae

9

African penguin

Penguins cannot fly in the air, but all penguins are birds and have wings. Their uniquely evolved wings are covered in scale-like feathers. These wings function like flippers that allow them to "fly" through the water. Penguins may spend up to 75 percent of their lives in the water. They are excellent swimmers and see and hear quite well underwater.

Some species of penguins will sometimes leap out of the water, seeming to fly through the air for a second or two. This is called "porpoising," named for the behavior that porpoises and dolphins often exhibit when they take breaths of air.

African penguins

Adélie penguins

★ This ability to leap high in the air is also used to get back onto land after a long day of hunting at sea. Penguins have been seen leaping as high as ten feet in the air to get from the water onto the ice or rocks!

Gentoo penguins

Rockhopper penguins

Humboldt penguin

- Most scientists believe there are 18 different penguin **species**. Almost all have the familiar black and white "tuxedo" look. This coloring creates a type of camouflage when the penguin is in the water. When a predator sees the white belly of a swimming penguin from below, they have a hard time distinguishing it from the sky above.

  Some **species** also have bright colorful feathers on their heads, as well as colorful **eyes**.

Yellow-eyed penguin

Royal penguin

12

Blue fairy penguins

★ The only **species** that is not black and white is the little blue penguin. They are also called blue fairy penguins. These birds are born with blue feathers. Even their **eyes** are blue.

Blue fairy penguins

Blue fairy penguins

- Blue fairies are very noisy birds, capable of making many different noises. They squawk, roar, grunt, bray, and hiss. The young chicks make a high-pitched beeping sound.

  These penguins spend the day hunting for fish, then return to shore at dusk. At night they are often tucked in their burrows, hiding from the many land animals that prey on them.

Blue fairy penguins

Blue fairy penguins

★ The smallest penguin species is the blue fairy penguin. These penguins only weigh about two pounds. That's about the same as a little kitten.

The biggest species is the emperor penguin. They can weigh up to 80 pounds. That's about the same as a very big dog.

Emperor penguins   Blue fairy penguin   15

Gentoo penguin feet

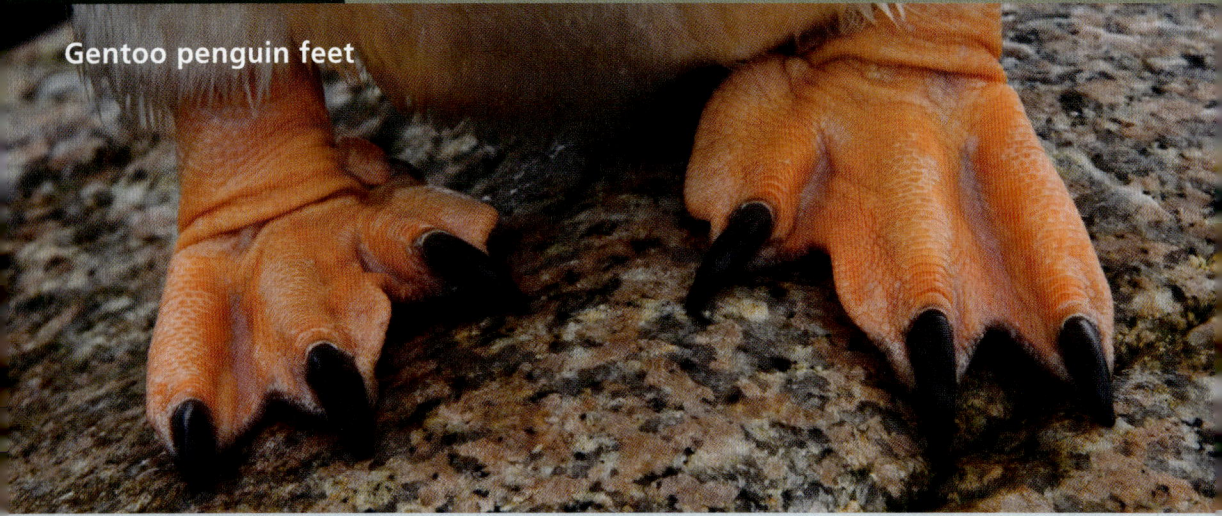

- All penguins have webbed feet, which are used like rudders to help control their direction in the water. Webbed feet, however, are not so great for walking. They are part of what gives penguins their trademark "waddle."

Gentoo penguin

★ Sometimes a penguin will lie on its tummy and push itself across the ice with its feet. It's faster than doing the waddle walk and it looks like it's a lot more fun!

Emperor penguins

17

Adélie penguins

Penguins are covered in tightly packed outer feathers which are coated with a type of oil to make them waterproof. Beneath them is an inner layer of soft down feathers. Under all those feathers is a thick layer of fat, or blubber. All of these layers help penguins to stay warm and **survive** in the cold ocean.

Once a year, penguins experience something called a catastrophic (cat-a-STROF-ick) **molt** where they shed their old feathers and then grow new ones. Most birds shed *some* feathers with each **molt**. Penguins shed *all* their feathers at the same time!

Yellow-eyed penguin molting feathers

Molting feathers, which will fall out and be replaced by new feathers

★   A penguin **molts** only once a year, but it can take two to three weeks. A penguin's slick oily feathers usually protect it from the freezing water of the ocean. While its feathers are molting, the penguin doesn't have enough protection, so it can't swim and fish during this time. Penguins must fatten up before they molt to **survive**.

CHAPTER 7

Chinstrap penguins
Antarctica

- All penguin species lay their eggs and raise their babies on land. Most species build nests together in a large nesting area called a rookery. A rookery can range in size from a few hundred to hundreds of thousands of birds.

  Different penguin species make their nest in different ways. Some make scrape nests.

★ A scrape nest starts with a shallow hole in the ground. The penguin then adds rocks, sticks, and anything else it can find. These nests look the most like a regular bird nest.

Rockhopper penguin egg

Gentoo penguin
Falkland Islands

●　　Mound nests are like scrape nests minus the shallow hole. These nests are usually built very close together. It is quite common for one penguin to steal material from another penguin's nest. This often sparks territory wars that can get very loud and nasty!

Another type of nest is the **burrow** nest.

Chinstrap penguins

Gentoo penguins

22

Magellanic penguin

★ There are several species of penguin that nest in **burrows**. The burrows may be caves or cracks in rocks or tree trunks. Six species of penguin use this type of nest.

Magellanic penguin

Blue fairy penguin

23

King penguins

Emperor and king penguins do not build nests at all. Instead, these "no nest" penguins nestle their eggs on their feet and keep them warm with something called a brood pouch. This is a patch of loose skin on their lower belly. The egg sits on the penguin's feet and is covered by this pouch to stay safe and warm.

Egg in
brood pouch

King penguins

Emperor penguin

★ The mother emperor penguin will lay a single egg. Then she must head out to sea to find something to eat. The father penguin stays behind to care for the egg. It takes about two months for the egg to hatch, but the father never leaves. Not even to eat.

25

Emperor penguin chicks

- When the eggs hatch, penguin chicks of every species look like little fluffballs. This fluff is cute, but not very practical. It is not waterproof, so the chicks can't go in the ocean to search for food. They must depend on their parents to survive for a **period** of time.

26   King penguins   Chinstrap penguins

Emperor
penguins

★   This **period** of time varies with each penguin species. It can last for as little as seven weeks for Adélie (ah-DEL-ee) penguins. For king penguins it can last for as long as a year!

Macaroni
penguins

Gentoo penguin

● During this time, one of the parents must go off to catch dinner for their child. This can take several days. How do they find their nest in the rookery when they return?

Scientists who study animal behavior **believe** that every penguin has a unique sound to its voice—just like humans.

Adélie and gentoo penguins

Gentoo penguins

Magellanic penguin

⭐ They **believe** the parent penguin can tell their own baby's voice from all the others. This helps them find the right nest with the right baby inside.

African penguins

29

African penguins

Humboldt penguin

• In many penguin species, a parent will feed their baby in a most unusual way. The parent will find and swallow the food, then hold it in their stomach for several hours, allowing it to partially digest. They will then regurgitate—or throw up— the partially digested food when they arrive back home.

Adélie penguins

Gentoo penguins

The parent opens its mouth. The chick puts its beak inside to get the food that has been thrown up. It may sound yucky, but it is the perfect meal for a baby penguin.

Emperor penguins

Gentoo penguins

Young gentoo penguin molting

Young king penguin molting

● As soon as the babies have grown big **enough** to leave their parents, they begin to molt. They will lose those fluffy feathers and waterproof feathers will replace them. Penguins who are going through this process are called fledglings. Once the young penguin has fully fledged, it must venture out of the safety of the nesting area and head for the open sea to find its own food.

Young African penguins molting

King penguins

★ Most young penguins will stay at sea and the nearby shore for three to five years. Then it is time to go back to the nesting area. They are now old **enough** to start a family of their own.

Chinstrap penguins

- Moving away from the nesting area to become an independent penguin is a dangerous but necessary part of becoming an adult penguin. There are many different **predators** in the waters where they look for food. These include killer whales, sharks, sea lions, and **leopard seals**.

Killer whale chasing gentoo penguin

Leopard seal

★ **Leopard seals** may look cute, but they are the main **predator** of many penguin species. Their teeth are very sharp, and they are very fast swimmers.

Leopard seal

Gentoo penguin captured by leopard seal

● There is so much to learn about penguins. Here are just a few more fascinating facts.

Penguins in Antarctica often huddle together for warmth. The penguins inside the huddle are heated by those around them. They rotate often to

Emperor penguins huddling

give every penguin a chance to warm up in the middle.

Penguins swallow a lot of ocean saltwater, but they have a special gland above their eye that filters salt from their bloodstream. They then expel the salt through their nose— by sneezing!

King penguins huddling in snowstorm

Gentoo penguin rookery
Antarctica

★ Lots of penguins in one place means lots of penguin poop. All that penguin poop stains the ice a dark color. This big, dark ice patch can be seen from outer space.

Gentoo penguin rookery
Antarctica

Emperor penguin chicks

If you would like to learn even more about these delightful animals, there are many interesting videos available online. Ask a teacher or parent to help you look them up on a computer. It's a great way to see for yourself how they live and to hear how they sound.

Macaroni penguins

Magellanic penguins

★ The more you know about penguins, the more you are sure to love them!

King penguins

PENGUIN SPECIES

Gentoo

Snares

Macaroni

Chinstrap

Adélie

Royal

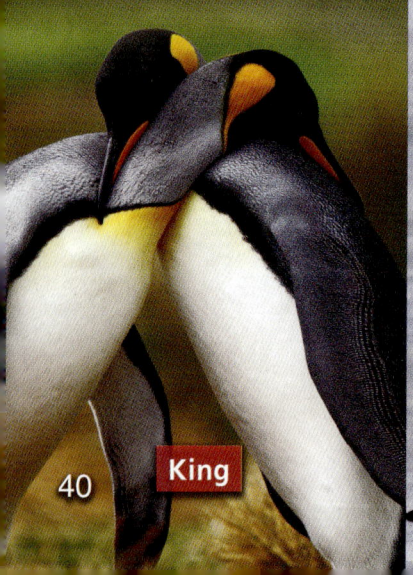
King

Emperor

Blue fairy

Southern rockhopper

Magellanic

Humboldt

Galapagos

Northern rockhopper

Yellow-eyed

Fiordland

African

Erect-crested

Glossary

Antarctica
the continent or land around the South Pole

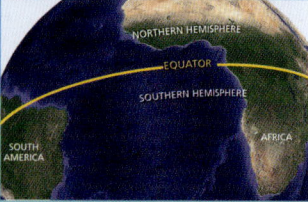

equator
the invisible line around the center of the globe that divides Earth into two hemispheres— Northern and Southern

krill
a small shrimp-like animal that is food for penguins

papillae (pe-PILL-lay)
the spines in a penguin's mouth that help the penguin to hold and swallow food

molt
the act of shedding old feathers

rookery
a collection of nests where penguins raise chicks in a large group

Questions to Ask after Reading

Add to the benefits of reading this book by discussing answers to these questions. Also consider discussing a few of your own questions.

1 Penguins are popular animals. Why do you think that is? What is it about them that appeals to so many people?

2 What are some of the physical differences between various penguin species? What are some things that are the same in all penguin species?

3 What are some of the different types of nests that penguins create? What do you think is the reason for these differences?

4 How do penguin parents take care of the chicks?

5 Can you name any animals that prey on penguins?

If you liked **Penguins** here are some other
We Both Read® books you are sure to enjoy!

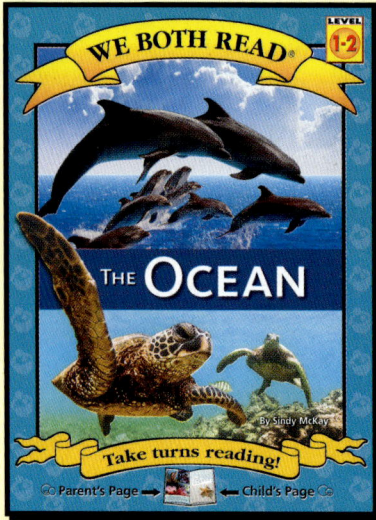

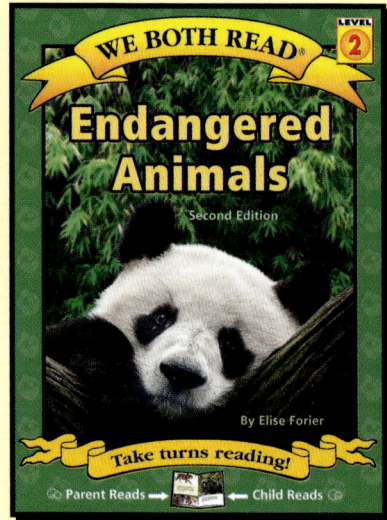

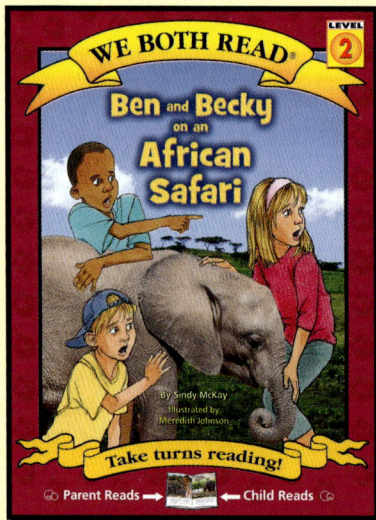

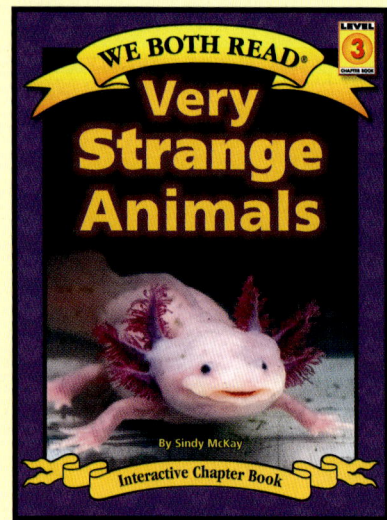

WE BOTH READ®
LEVEL 1·2
THE OCEAN
By Sindy McKay
Take turns reading!
Parent's Page → ← Child's Page

WE BOTH READ®
LEVEL 2
Endangered Animals
Second Edition
By Elise Forier
Take turns reading!
Parent Reads → ← Child Reads

WE BOTH READ®
LEVEL 2
Ben and Becky on an African Safari
By Sindy McKay
Illustrated by Meredith Johnson
Take turns reading!
Parent Reads → ← Child Reads

WE BOTH READ®
LEVEL 3 CHAPTER BOOK
Very Strange Animals
By Sindy McKay
Interactive Chapter Book

To see all the We Both Read books that are available,
just go online to **WeBothRead.com**.